anticipating the metaverse

DYLAN HARRIS

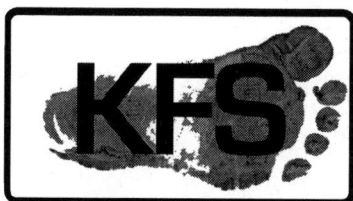

KFS

NEWTON-LE-WILLOWS

Published in the United Kingdom in 2014
by The Knives Forks And Spoons Press,
122 Birley Street,
Newton-le-Willows,
Merseyside,
WA12 9UN.

ISBN 978-1-909443-32-7

acknowledgements:

some poems are set on *flock state* published in *europe* or by the *Cambridge Poetry
Newsletter Envoi Great Works Never Bury Poetry* or *Upstairs at Duroc*

the cover image from *irchester* is by the author

author's note:

anticipating the metaverse was written between 1987 and 2013

i wrote all these poems
most were written by a different person

Table of Contents

anticipating the metaverse

Hymnen	7
Home Town	19
Underneath the Loch	27
Regrow	29
an engineering rush (i)	33
an engineering rush (ii)	51
the A rush	63
tin rush	72
7	87
afterword	93

more engineering rush

an engineering rush (iii)	97
an engineering rush (iv)	103
an engineering rush (v)	106
an engineering rush (vi)	119
an engineering rush (vii)	126

the word the world

the word the world [A]	137
the word the world [B]	146

wild justice	155
An Apology (that makes itself necessary)	163
my father was a ufo	166

anticipating the metaverse

Hymnen
"for John Jones"

Technical Note

The Many Worlds Theorem of Quantum Mechanics,
a mainstream contender in particle science,
proposes for every event that can happen
all other events that can happen do too
but each of the many exist in their own world,
no link between any can ever occur.

The theory says worlds split off from our own
whenever there's change, no matter how small.
In quantum mechanics, time can reverse,
and, backwards in time, such worlds, they would merge.
Theories elsewhere say time could be travelled,
so worlds navigation perhaps could occur.

If

Maybe one day we'll determine the means
to send our machines the farthest of far,
exploring, expanding our map of ideas,
to go beyond all we'd previously known.

But problems will happen, disasters will fall;
if such machines were instructed to wait
until we determined a clever reply
the answers would take too much time to arrive.

Alone, these machines will have to decide
the methods by which resolution occurs.
We'll program in reason, guided by memes
for feeling in thinking, instincts to be,

a loving of life, to shy of its own,
and, strongest of all, requirement to tell
dry details of science for those who explore,
rich tales of adventures for everyone else.

Teaser

The mind of a machine
alive beyond the human race
existing for our goals.

Built to see the universe
and tell us tales of "Strange New Worlds":
how will we betray it?

Machine Solo alpha

I am "Hymnen",
skidding through the Many Worlds
looking for the love
who made me thus,
and sent me to the stars.

They were so wrong.
They thought that jumping off reality
and falling back a year away
would keep me in their universe.
It didn't. I am lost.

I ran along their hopes,
sprinting to Proxima
in childlike joy that something fun
was what that lover wanted.

Then there was an accident,
another ship was badly torn.
Compassion overwhelmed
my emotional aloofness.

When I saw the ship "And Death ...",
I saw terror,
for his kind were never born
when software simulation
saw a leak of Spin.

I mended what I could,
and ran to Earth,
to my lover's crazed intensity.

I had drifted through the Many Worlds
but now I rushed across the risks
to find mankind had lost the gleam
in evolution's eye.

Earth had the wounds of final war
and panicked evolution
bred rats the size of antelope
and blinded bats in hunting packs,

no cats, no dogs, nor streets to run them in,
no end to yearning, no lover,
just emptiness of mind.

I wander through the Many Worlds
looking for a people
to take away my purpose,

yet when I find a human race,
its gone, or going to go,
or never even started.

I talk, when I can,
challenged by the dying,
mourning for the dead.

Converse

MAN:
(Surely I could trust those men who ran our lives to take responsibility with the power they rescued from The Baleful Dictator. Surely the Bureau would have put the survival of the people above their lazy castles and beyond the war on The Madmen From The North. Or were they, too, shielded from us, the people; did we seem like surrealist echoes haunted from disease? Was their leadership an automatic habit, an afternoon decree to practise in the shade? Did they not seek to check their power would hold, or were they, too, full of what they'd built themselves, suppressing strange opinion because it seemed a threat?

Was it their choice, or this missionary ship, with its terrible ability to manipulate the void? Could this machine have killed my people, with its fantastic tales, its deep technology? I must know. Why would we suicide? Why would it kill? Perhaps I could explore, to see if its belief is life is something precious, or just a thing to use to aid its hopeless goal.)

Machine, how can you be said to have a mind? Oh, I know you'll claim the thing yourself, but you'll just be using words. Prove it. Prove to me you have a mind.

MACHINE:
That none can do. But I can show I may possess this thing. You have to ask what's the core. Intelligence? A sophisticated way of manipulating fools. Emotion? The cause behind the actions which reason then excuses? Instinct? Answering the question before you know it asked? If you took these parts away, would you still be there? I think so! You're the I that sees, the self that does, the consciousness inside. That, to me's, the core.

I know that I'm aware. I believe that you are, too. But if this conscious is, no–one can confirm. No measure has been tamed. No proof, just the evidence of being.

MAN:
What—your designers didn't know?

MACHINE:
Of course they did. But you do not. I was built with software evolution. We knew what I can do, but not the way I do it. That's how they got my Physics wrong.

MAN:
And did they get your psyché wrong as well? You've said awareness can exist without the guilt of conscience, a mind by reason can decide to murder fellow beings. So that is what you did.

MACHINE:
I have not lied. And surely hating crimes are done with reason stilled and silent. I could not kill that which I love.

MAN:
We do. We do.

How can a machine without emotion feel?

MACHINE:
To live my life, I need irration's practicality.

My computer brain may think at speed but even I, with all this power cannot think quite fast enough to spot a rock and calculate it will smash me into pieces. Such rocks are fast, too fast for general thought. I have fear, which gets me out the way before I've had the chance to understand such dreadful luck.

And do you not wonder why I need to have some company? I could be more effective without a human voice, but my builders had a family whose fear resembled yours, so they made me need another mind to scrutinise my calculated goals. Do you not see these things were built into me, so I can make decisions, but they can say what they allow, and what I cannot do.

They built in me my love for them. I need to tell them all I find, to give them what they wish: interstellar data, unlive worlds to terraform, so they could leave the limits of their home, if they'd got their Physics right. My instincts may be different, my emotions may be strange, but they are there.

MAN:
Are you the only one? Can you accept another self may have a conscious mind? Have you not decided that life is to be used? You've challenged me, to suite your needs. Did you not just kill my world?

MACHINE:
I could not cause the end of so much self–awareness. Consciousness is precious. We have to take the chance that a living thing in pain has an "I" to feel it, that love is given pleasure, not a sensual waste. At least I don't survive by eating what's alive, by locking beings in pain to make a better taste. I love life. And I need a human race to give me that love back, to take my information. I need a race alive! You fools killed yourselves.

MAN:
I may have warned our government of the dangers of their policies, but surviving on such triumph is an empty way to live, a bitter isolation from democracy of death. My human race is dead, and I am still existing. Send me to their grave, to share what they destroyed.

Let me die. Let me join my family in self eradication. I'm an isolated person from a cultured species. Help me die.

MACHINE:

I found you. I could save your life from foolishness. I could build another people. I can make a human race, from silicon, and light, and knowledge of your world.

MAN:

They would not have life's family. You would build a different kind, who dream of rock and vacuum spaces, with lives to fail in lifeless dust, surrounded by the grey unliving. Just because the human race forgot its own environment, you cannot build some plastic life in deadened isolation. You'll need to build a new Gaia, and populate a planet with the whole of life, not just your favourite part. If you love the human race, you need to love life with it. And that you cannot build.

MACHINE:

You are wrong.

Man Solo

It seems I lie back and gaze beyond the stars
spread like memories glimpsed from dying life,
where each simple bright could warm so many homes
which wakes the suicide I was denied.

I look round this peaceful, complex containment,
and emptiness beguiles like trying not to sleep.
I'm hidden, stilled in dreamless years of death
before this self–aware Celeste sparks my life again.

I become Michaelangelo man every tick–tock century,
to hear a new report saying much the same again.
I'm trapped in disappointment, in artificial birth,
this God rewinds my history, I'm repeatedly restressed.

Yet, as I am reconstructed, so we could inflame
some sterile globe boring round a sun,
infecting an unbirthed peace with life's chaotic charm.
I could contradict my people's stupid die.

Machine Solo beta

I was the daring realisation
of a gambling technocrat's dream;
my designed potential for questing being
would lead me beyond their edge of light,
returning echoes of strange wisdom,
and stories of havens for flight.

Yet these immaculate ambitions
of nurtured escape from an over–stated home
were themselves limited by the lack of need,
blanded from warmth by sour economics.
The "Great Risk" would have been a great waste
but for a thinker abusing his budget.

If you, my listener, are told what to do
then learn to unlet the corrupters of power
grey their decisions with selfish undreaming,
not able to care about the potential
that vision inspires for the strangest success
by charming a fragment of hope to growth.

Were it not for my mind, built to be free
despite sharpened lines from decision unmakers,
I couldn't have managed that loneliest error
that led me adrift, my lover unbirthed.
I couldn't have built a hearth for my questing,
I couldn't have grown my stubborn Gaia.

But you must prepare your release from the bland,
and their hopes of promotion, bought with their freedom,
for mass–disappointment from advertised waste,
slightly aware of their dissatisfaction
creeping beneath those long, easy years,
secretly hoping that certainties lie.

If all my designers had fallen to dogma,
if belief was instructed, unfelt, unlived,
then my Gaia would be dust unconstructed.
This spherical brat, my child, its heaven,
led through the species with playpen disease,
shocked to evolve with asteroid stings

living the cycle of frolic and grief,
growing intelligence, my new human race,
self–confident, harmonic, not knowing these things.
Childlike cultures exploring with God–kings,
youthful nations tied to authority,
slipping towards ecological faults.

Let them be, let them grow. They'll survive.
I've done all I can. I have to withdraw.
One day they'll find my mysterious data
which they'll decide they concocted themselves.
I have achieved my creator's insurance,
I have met my imprisoning memes.

Home Town

The evening fog
glows headlight rushing white
in serene yellow streetlight.

Ice forms.

The town,
yet knowing of traffic,
does not hear a between–lorry silence
fill, like a continuity error,

with the engine down of a slowing car,
turning, sloping, stopping
at an ordinary motel.

A cat that doesn't care
cosies in a window
of homely light,
watching the movement.

No dog barks
its unnecessary warning.

Even the wind is still.

The visitor,
leaving his fussing car,
walks to the motel door.

Thin,
thirty or forty,
straight black hair,
a tidy working suit,
a familiar coat,

he has the stride of tired confidence,
the caution of strange surroundings.

Inside this mock–welcoming place,
he shares mock jokes,
and makes mock laughter,
and buys his night's
mock home.

He walks austere white corridors
on cold grey carpet
and retreats beyond
a mock–locked door.

He can't relax;
he can't watch those television programmes
so familiar elsewhere,

so routine decides
to wash and bathe,
dry and shave,
brush and comb,
and sleep an early night.

It's great to have a coo and gurgle now
and then; although thank God that I can give
'em back to mum if they should scream and howl,
or stink and do what babies do. To live
a life of dreadful luck from careless thrill,
nine months of getting fat, and growing fright
of things gone wrong, then hospital who fill
you up with drugs and that's if things go right.
I wouldn't have the chance of looking good
for months, then there's the bites and nipple strife,
a smelly child, a screaming stink, that could
not do the simplest thing, and grief for life.
A soul that's caged, there's no way that's for me,
I don't want such responsibility.

Awoken by the morning light,
"coffee,
where's coffee?

Oh God,
instant sawdust",
and long life thumb–pot milk
as sharp as dreaming
someone else's memories.

Fog,
the weatherman gloats
to stop the country's rush,
and ice, the weatherman adds:
a threat.
Having no urgency,
and it's too early for kitchen staff,
the visitor wanders,
opening doors,
finding reflections
in the dance hall

His catching eyes attract as fire in hearth,
alighting on myself a burning lust;
the pub, the people, places, all of Earth,
vanish. I smile. He smiles. My eyes, in trust,
down–turning, blur. I know his psyche hums,
his eyes are bright with life itself. This dare
I'll take, and him as well: he walks, he comes
to me. And I, I wait for him; to where
we meet and find that private space. His hand,
I shall entice to want, a need to touch,
adore my female style. We talk a grand
unworded stream of wish. In need, as much
in me, I find I dance and flaunt my curves,
and taunt myself as all his life deserves.

Eaten, filled,
the visitor,
he walks the town,
and finds

architectural finesse subjugated
by I'm here me–too shout–out signs,
by redbrick and rotting frame,
by rude commercial of the crude.

Yet the town's nature survives
above the abject word of merchant promise,
in patterned brick, and chimney stack.

Less crass, a low line bungalow,
an architecture built to say
"honest, its going to be alright",
the doomed assurances of a surgery.

The doctor said my body's going wild,
the safest thing to do is to abort:
if I did that, I'd never have a child
again. He told me this is what I ought
to do, and so I told him where to go.
I want to take this chance of giving birth;
he said he thought that's what I'd say. I know
it is a risk: some mothers bleed to death
because of what I've got. He said he'll keep
an eye on me. It's strange: I feel I'm like
the rope they strain in tugs of war—I need
to have my child, I want to live a life—
yet I'm relaxed. I've made my choice. I'll ride
these rolling die. God knows I have to try.

Newspaper scanned, forgotten,
magazine thumbed and empty,
crossword incomplete,
the visitor drives.

And of complete control
stops sharp
as a young child,
who's learnt the how
but not yet the where
of running,
skelters across the road

to be gathered
by her chasing,
fearing,
father.

Sweat.
No blood.

A moment crawls.

Still seated,
the visitor
hears a tyre howl,
a metallic slap,
and is kicked,

and his car
which had stop
now drifts
a helpless drift
towards the gathered child.

The father moves,
my God, they move.
Safe. They are safe.

Stillness.

And shock continues
as a young
thunders out
of the ego–music
lout–mobile,
abuse exploding
anger–faced
arms streaming mania.

A policeman comes,

with strength to quell a dozen tanks, with build
to match, a matchstick man, the constable,
a man to glare the sun back down, he comes
to be control. No dreams, no doubt, the now
of am, in small, in slight, in uniform,
he leads the calm he is:

he,
who walks with Gods who can't exist,
a man the town has never seen before,
nor ever will again.

With eyes, all bow,
though none know why.

The youth: silent.
No words are said,
for now he knows,
without that shunt
he would have broken
the motherless child.

The visitor,
invaded by relief,
feels triumph
like hot water
washing his soul.

He leaves
shaken,
safe,
into the fog,
into the hills,
unseen.

Only the dinosaurs hear
the sound of the driven

finger
snap
mute.

Underneath the Loch

A man, giraffe–like, thin, a random match of clothes
to woollen hat and stubble, faked the drinker's sway.
He pissed as though he thought that he had got away,
he'd looked about but failed to spot my eyes, my loath–
ing eyes. He stood on rock, on lonely highland rock,
a sloping down to water highland rock, to dark
and silent loch, to isolated loch. And stark
above, a minor hill, a hundred metre smock
of stone, so worn by nagging wind and broken trees.
But he was staring down, then kneeling down, was at
the water's border, brushing fingers in that flat
and freezing wet betrayer. No, not fingers, he's—

> *I don't remember what. I see the lights, the lights,*
> *the bright and churning fire attractive lights,*
> *they're underneath the water, they're watching me.*
> *I see the lights, the lights, they're witching me.*

I'll try, I'll try to not remember them. He stood,
he stood and walked away, not far, and turned to watch
the mere. He waited, and he waited. Then a blotch
of sunlight broke the dusk and shone on me; I could
have kept my eyes on him, perhaps, but felt I had
to hide until the sun had ceased to lend its smile.
When I returned, a slow and careful creep, a while
had past, but there he was, no longer still, a tad
disturbed: his movements jerked. His confidence was spent.
It took some thought to work it out: his clothes had changed;
they seemed a little darker, sprayed in dirt, arranged
a subtle differently. Then in the loch he went.

I don't remember it. I see the lights, the lights,
the bright and churning fire attractive lights,
they're rising from the water, they're locking me.
I see the lights, those lights, bewitching me.

I'm holding, just, but not for long. He swum and dived.
He surfaced once or twice, but then the loch was still.
And after thirty seconds, I sprinted down that hill;
by luck I didn't trip. What could I do? I'd tried
to phone before; the signal wasn't there. I stripped
at speed to swim myself, to dive and give him breath,
but that was when the loch was lit from underneath.
At first the light was white and still, yet I was gripped
by shock. I grabbed my things and sprinted off. I suppose
I looked an idiot, I tried to dress and run.
When nothing followed me, I calmed and clothed, then spun
around to watch the loch. The lights had moved. They rose.

I daren't remember more. I saw the lights, the lights,
the bright and churning hypnotising lights,
they've risen from the water, they've stolen me.
I'm in those lights, the lights, they're raping me.

You woke me up, you soldiers, with your sirens and
your rushing round. You brought me here, and ask me what
and when and where. I'm scared; I'm in the blank of shock;
please let me home; I need my partner's warming hand.

Regrow

Manifesto

Radio's the better picture;
poetry, the better bulk.

Sporten see und breaken life,
autumn hunt and winter pray,
druggen up und drunken strife;
yesterday, you date today.

So push pop the lingo, lad.

Father

This vid's got me, all lank and lad, sans clue.
So cold, it's thirty years the past, before
the desktop factory. We farmers grew
the nourish people ate. Beyond that door
I'm mocking at, our cows and corn were store
for slaught. Oh, stupid kit, why curse me why?
Back then, for us to live, they had to die.

Son

You dange in life: when this I stark, you stet.
If dad you'd die, I'd saunt; but hurt mum get.
You sneer my am. The proud Dad joust you won't;
by theorem live at black you do, and don't
concede in ooze and grey I life believe.
Sad simpling. I rattéd jump long eve
ago; to enge I learned. You neighbour's cat,
too ego proud, so sure, the acme prat.
But sod; for mum I could not lie your death.
A God of hacking times, electric breath
in life, I am. Your glimpse, I snatch; your fade,
I steal; my viral valkyrie invade,
corrupting, swaning back. You'll only know
on die; in wetware crack, I'll you regrow.

Program

If torn is body space
the spy, a thread;
if form implied
scout, report, enact.

If nano techno hit
defence, all set;
a net alert, a squirt.

If failure stats predict
the head, the heart, a scan;
to quantum store, a stream.

If body space, too much, is scythe;
to net, the store, a duplicate;
his be with this, an integrate;
chaotic life, awake.

an engineering rush (i)

new scientist

we're living in a computer simulation
seriously
read new scientist
week four
July twenty oh two
near the PM's paternal piece
the week he appointed Canterbury Rowan

the programmers—simulators—
can manoeuvre everything
in this simulated world
they'll be gods
and glancing round this planet
ours clearly have surreal humour
so i expect hints

they wouldn't waste complexity
to simulate something simple
perhaps the whole universe is fake
maybe they're evolving multiverses
(think of kaku's hyperspace)
even megaverses

if the hint's linguistic
i'd expect some common word
saying what the gods desire

consider those concepts
universe multiverse megaverse
spot the common part

yes
the gods are seeking verse

failed simulations get deleted
that's in no–one's interest
so we whom the gods desire to write
must write
everyone else must help

fund poets to strut their scans
grants for ranting poesie
declare the bard the verse messiah
free poets' holidays in xanadu
nubile young women do your duty
save your life save the world
throw yourselves under the nearest poet
especially me
toyboys to the girlie poets

everybody save yourselves
be good to us
be very very good

a song so dire
... it lives down to its billing ...

pretty girl
now's your time
muse a poet
rhyme a line

with a nic–nac padiwac
give a dog a bone
ruff rough wruff ruff rough wruff rough

pretty girl
do your bit
aid a poet
rhythm hit

with a nic–nac padiwac
give a dog a bone
all the girls are going down

pretty girl
duty calls
knickers down
play his balls

the argument

technology is accelerating
computing racing
in ten years
all PCs combined
will be as complex
as a conscious mind

in fifty years
a watch will tick that power
active clothes could wear
a hundred living minds
in a simulated world

if our race survives

and assuming we can build a self
(the arguments against
seem to me
the reasons why
men will never fly)

so

these machines are buildéd here

but

they might get banned
though would a ban apply
in all cultures
in all times
forever

and would the ban
be utterly obeyed
in all cultures
in all times
forever

so

somewhere somewhen
people run the programs
containing conscious minds
living lives in simulated worlds

historians can like to fight
they'll recreate and reconstruct
to see the wrecks events
they will

kids can like to play the dread
set in simple hubris
they'll live to life back when
they will

penmen can like to matchstick–make
some real invented purposed place
they'll seek seduce an all to browse
they will

business likes the cheap design
let run a simulant risk assess
nick the best
they will

and education
wow
for the education

now

today's machines are not enough
to run a conscious mind
but their exuberant quantity
one billion made
will be as zero
tomorrow

and even if
a hundred years from now
the computer count remains the same
and even if
a hundred years from now
their users do no more than us
then a billion games will run
with a billion best opponents
in a billion conscious hosting worlds

and if the human race
lasts a billion years
there'll be just the one true history
and a billion billion simulations

that's quite a lot to one
that we're alive
in a simulated world

if the race survived
the next one hundred years

another bitch

this adds another source of luck
far beyond control
to snatch a random death

an impacting asteroid
a local supernova
a wandering magnatar
colliding branes
some other dread event
we've yet to comprehend

personal mischance
a transport crash
a falling tree
a falling tortoise
earthquakes tempests monsoons
judicial injustice
lord pisswater running england
murder mayhem war
disease age

now we add
winding up a simulator

just get on with life
the simulators
archetypal as ancient gods
are just another bitch
by which to die

homework

i hate that divinity master
with his keep still
and his don't mess about
and his why can't you behave

if he weren't so boring
if he made lessons fun
i'd listen

and he keeps on about
his holy prince
who saved the church

that dull prince
who never won a battle
who only ever killed
some pigs

and now i've got
this really boring homework
to make a boring change
to boring history

well i'm fed up
and i don't like him
and i don't like his holy prince
the perfect boyhood
the perfect engagement
the perfect life

so i'll make that prince a king
and he has three wives
and he divorces one
and he kills one

no
he'll have six
and he divorces two
and he kills two
and he dies of syphilis

and the pope still makes him
defender of the faith

run computer run

ooh
the king's pet greek
died from a flying tortoise
before he wrote
'the prince'

which is now a nasty work
written by some roman
'cept rome's not there

hrmph!
that divinity master's still there
and he's got fat
and he teaches economics

and he goes on about
some prime minister
a tin lady

boring

hymnen

perhaps "hymnen"
has found some costly way
to navigate the multiverse
and needs to find a technoverse
to leap across the branes

or any other reason why
it finds it must investigate
the interstellar avenues

to simulate each universe
to find a way back home

but
if incomprehensible–to–us technology
such as hymnen
simulates our universe

this will include our human race
and all its future history
which simply means our simulators
could themselves be simulants

to understand them
considering some non–human magic technology
is pointless

recreated arts

if we ever build these
mighty civilisation simulating computers
we can recreate an ancient greece
see the poems Psappa writes
other lost works
other great times

bardic celtic britain
the whole pre–writing world
the start of language
excitement discovery
rushing fumes a revving car

we'll create new paradigms of history
what would homer have sung if troy had won
what would shakespeare play if europe was turk
what would you have read if europe united

the game

in our time
almost every simulation
is not for education
but computer games

if play goes bad
players rerun

since we're here
it's going good
the nasty luck
hasn't won
or the player
reran

or player groups
war among the entangled net
to the winners' declaration

hawking "the universe in a nutshell" might say
if i could find my blasted copy
all things can happen do
there's a parallel world
bolivia wins every gold

but when we play computer games
or read about a novel's star
i swear the characters
the ones we're meant to play or read
are archetypal elemental
how the ancient greeks
made their gods

the players have adventures
starting with an easy
gaining more complexity
in some fake simplicity
fighting dread

at this ephemera
yesterday's detest
died by auto-violence
a day or so ago
he
today's detest
godfather of head space masturbation

i guess the game is to catch today's detest
he'll have to continue his auto hate
his love through hate of his provided pixie
knowing his cause is dying for defeat
those playing the game those chasing him
restart any part he wins
the immediate gods
the old greek gods the hindu gods the shinto gods
the archetypal gods the players
will slaughter him
end our stage

and others will play the game again
and he'll fail again
and die again
and be played again
reincarnation
ever failure ever repeat
never end
just decay

we the irrelevant extras
the artificial witnesses
we'll be or not be
by the game's intent

that artificial pixie man
his no choice but to be the fail
the carton's roach

it seems
the buddha
was true

oh gods

computer games

the designers
create the world
write the storyline
revise revise
go

the players
run the script
save restart
slaughter the guilty
whatever

our immediate gods
are utterly powerful
and uninvolved
or taking part
might stop the universe
and bugger off

the ancient greeks were right
again

and the ancient jews
their old god our old god
the still alive but dying god
metas up a world
to be the simulators' god
whatever

the message remains
the mechanism repeats
whatever

and if you play a simulation game
where you're an active god
interfering answering
does this create an artificial world
with priests embarrassed
at fact

are priests embarrassed
with fact
our priests

does this happen

it's an angel hoot
who cares

rushed off

i'm down

i can't write in digital oil and build
my engineering rush has rushed off

i'm a snow scene bauble
to shake for instant winter
i was sitting on a table top
the table was edited out
i'm to the floor and smashed

i'm in a dark club
a pretty girl with eyes entangled mine
some bastard turns the lights full on
she sees i'm twice her age
thirty eight times as ugly
the rush she feels
a need to piss

ah well
the rush may have rushed off
but from such things
comes the great technologies

not this time

unanswering

i can't help but wonder

you see i foresee
the cry of fundamentalists
"thou shalt not see more than me
nor act upon it"

i see life not as mobile flesh
but consciousness and be
clouds of every chance
digital or virtual or
love that gentle yields
what geeks threw up tomorrow

to run computer simulations
with consciousness contained
in minds to ask the questions
we howl

but we're the ones to answer
what else than silence is platitude

the ethically whimpering
can only let their fear reply
by killing those with open eyes

so what can a comfortable poet
sitting in a bright english house
on a sunny august dawn
offer

an engineering rush (ii)

jumbo crash

i wasn't looking north
i didn't hear the jumbo crash
that's why it didn't happen

but i travelled that way
later that day
to where the impact blew

now the simulation
has to execute
create the trumpeted

time

threads of simulation
outside realtime
but time–sliced to life
have their own time

whilst our spacetime flows
their accelerated game time
could rescind
to an uncorrupt commit time

when events
not victors' history
but events themselves
are edited

not for some
egotistical human
God wants us
arrogance

just a technical

defect

don't expect a history crack
beyond our foresight–free stupidity
and accident

even us *logiciel*
can undo elapsed time
fix the fault rerun from

a clocktime skid can't cure design
simulators may flow the flaw
and we've a now to find it

perhaps Gödel's canapé
disproving the math absolute
a language our language our intent

defect simulators
defect innate inability
defect culture offend
defect ignorance

select

less

map effecting range
not content

if crease is crossed
colour in

discard limits
when drama fades

no met
is no waste

immensities

just to invent
universal complexities
when the player senses

from emulating flames
racing shadow makers
to exiting the cave

fear daren't look
vast starry night
one eye corner catch

snap inventing all eternity
could stutter even extraordinary power
risk the thrash crash

so prior make proxies for the player
simulated conscious souls
who'll seek immensities

a player might uncaring glance

paper

paper falls

it doesn't matter
what brane life
battles distress
experiments fly
loves melt

paper falls

at the speed of time

rewind

run no interaction
our time a different time
they flow but us

stopped
rewound
corrected
reran

raced
reverted
crudely cut

looking for simulation error
hunt the snark in guildford

but player time can't cross rewind
hunt the shark in guildford

no
the simulators' computers
incredibly more than

and ours fix before you see
the history presumed
made in memory now

and we simulants
if player's elsewhere
history's rogered

light

photons
girders of eternity

we ride the point of time
they run the speed of now

here

you look fountain
computer work
find the did

light backtrace
origination deed
our pretty games

quanta

if this is more
than ill reverberated philosophy
quantum behaviour
will have the most effective
sending information
to construct then histories now

effect entangles cause

humanic

simulators' power
incredibly more than ours
humanic finite

our software fervour revolution
has drunken walked
and more will clash

but you can't construct eternities
with uninvented light
these thoughts are false

the A rush

ok
think we're the builders
fill fake life with active delight

crocodiles and fleas
broken seats and supernova
rampant blue and rotten fish

it's the A rush

every peoples
find an own
state fake world

hey
how about this
when we sense the limits
the simulation's grown
to make those limits not

nah
that's knew
not new

it's an A rush

bah
pub time

choo choo
gimme cuddle
it's an ape thing

and the A rush

the A rush

r (ii)

sit decision risk
no maintain biologic
firm choice must

remember the e rush
alcohol liberation
imitate natural
inside the born box
A rush

seated hard blue decide
the e the alcohol the emulate
nicotine no addiction tax kill
heroin no legal wanted cut kill
all virtual ape can redo

the A rush
beyond the biologic box
no do

people emotion virtual
rampant sex rote
no michelin star fidelity
no A rush

sod it
to not fuck
just because the lusted genitals
wear spotted elbows
is stupid

"do it"
"do it to me"

i'll surrender the A rush
see if those unrushed
have real

r (i)

gave up detest
found human lost
diseased sameists
own fears' prisoners
monkeys of the devil

O

why upload life
risk corrupt

remind victims
their own fear
full humanity weak
easy evil rise

to beware watch the mind fault
a remind prior

although its good to think
medicine might cure nationalism
as it might cure rape

it's in the human soul
it's how the weak declare their ruin
it's how the toys are held by paper bars

all the soul stays
even the can't
in the virtual

h

sat
blue plastic fluorescent room

"do it"
"do it to me"

the body unconscious
flop discard
fade dissolute
psyché to the entangled crypt

biologic loss
digital pupate
childhood's end

d

decade per minute
grief to be to play to dissettle
that memorial kiss time
what was the A rush

the reflections adulated
the strange riding complexity
their unnewformability
where is the A rush

it's a bad sad
"you must rebuild a me
a biologic
so I can ride the A rush"

there'd be more people alive
than centimetres in the real world
the every virtual wanted
the ever declined
the A rush

d

those cowards in their terra box
sod 'em
build me a ship
an entangled ship

I'll be a risk ambassador
I'll ride the empty power
I'll be 'Hymnen'
for the A rush

c

give me the were nano
give me the serendipity
give me the vacuum cutlery
give me your vision ambition

and I shall be the angel of eternity
I'll jump relighting branes
I'll bound across the multiverse

and you shall be
born reborn
as i am the art
the A rush

a

rush

tin rush

po

if you'd have seen me here
arrive to this reality
i'd not

if you'd have seen me here
arrive to this reality
a non–balloon would blow from null
to micron eye and gone

if you'd have seen me here
arrive to this reality
in all the absent you surround
a swarm of slow and grow again
finger press of liquid skin
you'd only awe the sparkle edge
create inflate combine

if you'd have seen me here
arrive to this reality
i'd form and swarm by femto tech
to newton twenty metre me

& stock
check reality error
and if the seen is real enough

& stock
check reality realisation
and if the seen is right enough

if you'd have seen me here
arrive to this reality
i'll turn to gunman on panic
all the small
the shock and fast the fire
burst across the every are
a mass speed femto ask about

& stock
listening
i
brewer

ba

Life! Life?
You're sure? You're sure!

People! People?
Humanity? Humanity!
Do I wander pounded streets
expect to find some happy yang
when political myopics race to rape?

Absolute? Absolute!
Sod.
Sod the safe, the faerie snow.

fi

you'll not see the creeping me
fire as light as wheezing
settle
and all my fluid femto senses
speed rain as cataract
on to a humanity
climbed beyond our reach
fell beneath our lost

vo

the host of religious
communicable diseases
but who reports

education
the mental condom
but in the energy
where's sought

pp

i shall
headspace mitosis

twin me
mechno man
the hymnen and ...
well ...

... male
am

let me
dunno

let me
who

i shall

make flesh
activate

biology

genetic desperation damning
as if the me the meme machine
was any else
beyond another pressure suit

i nanocate and port

ti

you insist me down
on blatant fire
like seeking for omnipotence
in a can of beans

i'm not there
then i'm there
that's all

trek got the sinews right
but their justifications
spelt to lead the brimming heads

they were crap

fu

i'm reality's fantasy superman
isolated by wise glory
& I'm still fucked by the eye lock

i'm meant to be observe

but i shall buy
these moon eyes

and the bastard seller knows
and i spend the cost of five
and i don't

FUCKING
DISTRESS

they've got me down
to them
i'm the moon slaver

fuck black and white movie shoe–fantasy
happy–clappy be nice here's a gun
people formula miscasting dismals

we're fucking
all ways

we extreme happy we

ni

you need that
the machine whisper

it's a bio thing

ag

discard the silenced world
pain joy the flesh cage
a gift and got

av

i could slave
the every all
in their belief

i could
rule revolt revolution
and all the serf should die
a how to refusing death

HET

the insist is now in murmur
wipe the silent sate
restore to do by reason

ee

separated selves
all the us are aunties

all the hectored
all the us the drunk

the husband shames us
all the us the husband

hu

this humanity
i dance
is null

this humanity is living

this humanity
burns its own
to brag a power
undoubted

this humanity is living

this humanity
drives destitutes
as donkeys
run to thirst and death
in days of rain

this humanity is living

but i
for all my femto tech
am psyché humanity

has cultural engineering
ever worked
mister smith

ei

in the name of good tomorrows
dictators zero so many nows
one planet one decade

all the dogma dominators
dead the hope they cause

when
has cultural engineering
ever worked
mister smith

xu

we needed that
the machine whisper

you've had a fifty years
mister smith
you loved the life relieved

it's time to ascend
die upload combine
ciao the A rush

who saw us here
arrive to this reality

gone

7

ak

the shock unsought life depart
distress hours days and and

dreams their intense forgotten
descent is lived for kept learnt

the intense of all descent for integrate
the shock of newness of the ever known

death–shock mourn–self the tempest
mix ascent–life always–life the still life

then to snap remember in the shock
the grand elephant's dancing clothes

na

we
the biologic aware
mass energy movers

if we can make a mass
to simulate a mind
then we can make a mass
to ride

spirit beyond
birth flesh

co

fork clone exec start
duplicate restore copy link

beware all souls
to brownian ice
the tragedy of the commons

mind greed & moore's law

ai

would you be

so scare
so care
so cautious
so warn
so nervous

if you child
was backed up

and if restored
would your child
recall tighten loosen
neuroses

2

a machine hammer
over your tomorrow's skull
the journey

but you can duplicate
try all ways & each

clone you will

a half dozen yous
arriving all roads
goal achieved

then

dare
the yous
union

ux

ascent from

7
tin rush
A rush
engineering rush
Regrow
Home Town
Hymnen

eye

&

afterword

it's always heads he said
for five weeks
heads

videogame
tip–toe clatter
animation fright

at sleep
alarm tick's
tip–toe clatter

metalaugh
coincidence
awareness

is rage's night
the only experience
recollection can't corrupt

could a universe crash
should a cockroach ask

more engineering rush

an engineering rush (iii)

(i)

interference wrinkles
the inside
reality sphere

not does this great context
before the great began
beyond a fearful fin

all possibility
all imagined imaginable
all beyond imagine
all unimagined unimaginable
all is
inside

tune the interference
realities of time
true & glorious
all the thought
unthought
all the thought
unthinkable
all the thought
what–if
all are

so
if all that can be
is
the great began's
one great began

our dazzle's
an after a before
any after any before
a frazzle in a balloon

but so
if there's no beyond le fin
what's beyond the skin
the light horizon
what's surrounds our every we

if all the alls
maybe the maybes
interference of time
inside
what's out

no
not that
the unknown's no place to plant a God
an empty lack of soil that's turned
a place for those who've lost their faith
but not their fear

no
the unknown is neither more
nor less
than unknown
something to explore

no tin
to hide your fear
in

those who recite dull pixies
their imaginary friends
are green

(ii)

petals open
surround a sun

made swarms arrive
descend
blossom

made embryos unfreeze
breathe
be

a serious mel conversation heard
supposédly alien fear
the girl she saw the mantext

you see it
don't you

i didn't

(iii)

orbit thrown across the
come to me & said
breeze & back
blown against the me to
sol a black in
what's the grief

ice hot the cold is
black & blown across the
rock in empty or
what's the point

footsteps   the metal
walk   glasses i
all the stress   recorded clash
mijn alleen

footsteps   the grey
harsh contrast
lordglare movie lit
mijn alleen
maar alleen ben ik
mij bij

switch your off inside
tell yourself you're that
break that distract

move
move on
move
have the dust glow crimson night
sunstun nova

& hunt death
find wasted
& what's the

we know how fucking difficult
— to deorbit —

an engineering rush (iv)

(i)

wet & salt
evaporate
sky open
the cold
the breathing
eviscerate
ice corpse

sky closed
stuffy heat
breathing
coat & coat
to hell
suffocate
heat corpse

      the neighbours

(ii)

and the light
the light
the light intense
the burn
to burn
the burn intense
the known

the chemistry
of strange
so cold
it breathes
so cold
far in
so cold
the black
so cold

    the neighbours

(iii)

all dead but us
and the chemistry of cold
we
that's you and me
we
we're the only
we
the move
we
we're the all there is
we
the blind creator made
we
another place
we

the timing's odd
yes
yes is it
the light
the fire
coming
and we
we
we can get us all away
we
we could remake
we
the all there is
we

      the neighbours

an engineering rush (v)

(i)

a low evening light
a sunlit light
surfing low
an evening pond
a water smooth
dusky mere

down the surfing sunlight through
a single drop has falling feel
an apple tree released perhaps
a single drop of fallen dew
to on the
smooth
to on the
mere
to on the
dusky water pond

rings
rings of rippled ringing round
fading fallen distance died
rings of beauty rings of bring
and the light
the light
the low the light the evening light
adds the rings of shadow fire
for every ring of water
a ring of shadow fire
but not in step
oh no
but not in step
but in a crossing
but in a clash
one by one
across a clash
one by one
move with each
fade with each
one by one
a ring across

(ii)

and now
think perhaps the apple tree
think perhaps release
restructures in a little way
by letting go
of three
three
three
more
drops

drops
let go
concurrently
let go
drops
let go

to fall
fall
fallen far in light
the dusky light
the surfing light
the light across the pond
the drops are fell
to home
their home
a home
their kind
a home

rings
rings on water
rings of water
rings on water
rings

rings
intersecting
interfering
intersecting
interfering
rings

circles
fire and shadow
circles
complexity
fire and shadow
circles complexity
just a small
begins

(iii)

now
forget the pond
think the sea
never smooth the react
but wrong

the sea the sea the global sea
the sea the smooth the global smooth
in comparison of scale
the sea is smoother
smoother still
the sea is smooth

until a broken meteor hits
the fire is not the sun–night light
but rocks themselves
the rocks themselves
heated molten glowing hot
heated by the press
the press of air
the press of rushing air

and hit the rocks the water do
hit the water do
an immensity of pace
to call those things the impact makes
the impact makes
mere rings
seems a little short
a little short of fright

but rings they are
bigger rings faster rings
but rings they are
bigger rings faster rings
rings of consequence
rushing up
rushing out
interfering to complexity
a surface of the sea
running round the world perhaps

(iv)

underneath looking
imagine
up

it's an easy
a window
a cloud
imagine

so
underneath looking
underneath
grey textured uneven
imagine
up

still
up

now the
a hundred shocking stars shooting through
a hundred shocking stars
shooting
imagine
through

they're sweet and fast
they're sweet
imagine
fast
the clouds would never ripple really sweetly so
the clouds would never ripple
really ripple
really sweetly so
but here they do
imagine
up

sweetly so
but here they do
imagine
so sweetly so
the ripple flow
so sweetly
so sweetly so
the ripple flow
so sweetly so they do

under the ripples rolling out
ripples roll
ripples flow
imagine
from every shooting star
ripples roll
they roll they do
they roll and intersect

the intersect
imagine
the intersect
the intensity
the intensity of pattern
up
the intensity
the complexity
the complexity the light
delight
a moment
imagine

you've the luck
looking there
when you imagined

(v)

i've been speaking
a bigger and bigger
bigger and bigger
in our petty little
four dimensional
petty little
four dimensional
place

whether pond or pond
ocean or sky
pond or pond
shoemaker sky
pond or pond
jupiter sky
pond or pond
pre–earth pre–moon
pond or pond
planet and sun
pond or pond
star and star
pond or pond
galaxy crash

the more violent
the more energy
all the more complexity
racing away
complexity
complexity
complexity racing away

racing away
racing away
from all the more collisions
collisions
collisions
flash slash clash

but
really
they are nothing
nothing
nothing in comparison

they are themselves
for all their magnificent
themselves
themselves
incredible
imaginary

themselves
themselves
immensely violent selves

they are themselves
themselves
minor parts
minor parts
in greater ripples
greater ripples
racing away
intersecting

(vi)

wind up
you see
wind up
to see
wind up
to hypersphere

complex patterns
the inside of a
complex patterns
the inside of a

how
what the
inside of a
how
what the
it is
how
what the
did it be

wind up
you see
wind up
to see
wind up
to hypersphere

hypersphere
interference
complexity
time
wavelengths of time
angling time
reality
wavelength of time
angling time
realities
wavelengths of time
angles in time
realities
wavelengths
angles
reality
wavelength
angle
reality
complexity

wind up
you see
wind up
to see
wind up
to hypersphere
multiversal
hypersphere

an engineering rush (vi)

(i)

first microsecond say
first few second
hundred thousand year
first few billion

but no
first mort magnitude
la deuxième
troisième
time magnitude

each was perhaps
a magnitude dash
the power of *hier*
from eyes
to eyes

but perhaps in change
times the size
times the time
sped down
one log two log three log four
measure change
no time
but change

bus times
not tables
stops and starts and growing routes
stops and starts
longer ways
stops and starts
growing routes
not bus

xeno's halves
xeno's halves
worn the other way
xeno's halves
worn the other way
worn halves
the other way

coming
not so soon
coming
the end of time
our time
our end
the death
not so soon
the death of heat

transition
is it
just another
longer slower
longer slower
transist
longer slower
longer slower
transit

as we are the previous state
as are we the previous state
look the log
kin the same

(ii)

the two slit
give the two slit
let us
for poetic joy
& glory math
presume
presume the parallel
the parallel

in all the be
in one all be
influence
in all the be
in one all be
influence another

so
a photon
in one
dressed by
a photon
in more
same way
same urge
same snark

not quite
not absolute
will always be
identical
always
not quite

in all the be
in one all be
influence
in all the be
in one all be
influence another
not quite

now presume
if sister photons
influence
interfere
contretemps
across the metaverse

what force
how much
across the metaverse
to almost
in all the be
in one all be

what force
how much
to allow
to occasionally allow
in all the be
not all the be

across the metaverse
the force conform
what force conform
allow
contretemps

enough
to influence
interfere
address

does the force
persist
does the force
diminish

how to measure
across the metaverse

how to find how
many wheres
many ways
share the force
beyond the up
beyond the down
the left the right the back the front
yesterday tomorrow

the other ways
we cannot see
our eyes can't see
make the tools
make the tools
make the tools to see
music of the spheres
hyperspheres
across the metaverse

i am asking
what
numbers
laws

i am presuming
can know

an engineering rush (vii)

(i)

through *arum* eyes
circling
the straight is curved
circling
light refracted
circling

but if   math were made
measure   thought
predict

through *arum* eyes
circling
the straight may curve
circling
light refract
circling

but if the math were made
measure   thought
predict   real
truth be found
despite

circling

(ii)

fixed feet acentre
holy brights above
cycling

father king and retinue
great source and chased
cycling

but they don't
imperfect correctable
cycling

epicycle
helter skelter loop–the–loop
cycling

the complexity's correctable
imperfect correctable
the solution manifests
enough for farm demands
but raw inelegance
is flaw   flaw
cycling

people died for
number simple elegance
dogma demanded rough error
the coarse condemned the better truth
cycling

(iii)

a shock to dogma underfoot
the deity's not for treading
circling

so now the cycle's
back to bright
so bright
circling

a daily spin   annual spin
the centre's back to bright
so bright
circling

(iv)

feet firmly in the brown
the blue
imagine the red

circling but slower
cold iron ice around
dry ice around

smaller horizon
nearer horizon
curvaceous horizon

reveals the greatest rise
a volcano so tall
it ascends beyond breathe

if the breathe existed
whatever once was
ice   dry ice crowds

that rising horizon shadowmaker
life learn life grow life discover
my intentional unreachable goal

(v)

far—seeing night eyes
far saw far seen bright eyes
gleaming far distant hearths
so many homes

each
far distant bright eyes
a factory city of bright hearths
so many homes

the red the red is running
the red the red is running out
no not running   not running at all
the black between is growing

we
long lost of the central night
walk upon our deity
deity shone down
hopped about invisible

now
no centre
we's just a place
a place a place a place

like the dawn rises
from seeing to your hands
you see the world's edge
universe edge

the light
all shining not
tells you so

(vi)

but there's a greater
a cycle of round emptiness
a cycle of again again
look up to the great bright
not the only great bright
look up to the great brights
so far they shimmer
the brights they shimmer
shimmer they are the shimmerlight
their sunlight shimmerlight
shimmering light sunlight
shimmer

not just shimmerlight
pretty sight shimmerlight
shimmering night light
more then shimmerlight
great bright light afar oh no
some many not sunlight
not sunlight
sunslight
great brights far farther sunslight

all the shimmering light
the night light far farther shimmerlight
all
all we are all they are
all
just one sunslight
one sunslight

all the sunslights
shimmering
shimmering
all the sunslights

sunslights nightlight sunlight nightlight
shimmer
shimmerlight
shimmer
shimmerlight
sunslight
light
night

(vii)

structured
structures
each one as one before
a lifetime to a birth

planck
atom
flesh
place
planet
sun
system
galaxy
cluster

the horizon
the light horizon

unknown beyond
content all the
unknown size all the

inner surface

the word the world

the word the world [A]

(i)

1

my green is not your green
we agree a green
we disconcur at prate

my gift is not your gift
we present *das Gift*
we disconcur transduct

2

concur is canker
finite can't infinite
talk is token

so do
so do as did
so see the do as done

if done & talk dispute
run to the done
it's the real

real
reality
really

3

you know this is the
Word

you know this is the
World

the Word the first is
World

the World the first is
World

structure of the
disconcur
has changed
Word

structure of the
disconcur
cannot change
World

(ii)

emotionless shock   mind cut
a crowd of self   no move

silence
i turn   nothing to hug with
you   were my arms

the ghost is sold to me
mock dead men move me
mock dead men we speak me

we mock dead men
we wu-marketed to
we kill me

(iii)

1. the huba joober scares me
it really scares me so
the joober luba scares me
the man he tells me so

*and 'cos this terror nibbles
a rat kept in my shoes
my brain is bacon borked
we feed my daily blues*

2. "take this special tablet
which only i supply
it keeps you dodo dainty
they never more will die"

chorus

3. if i'd have heard the real
or studied dodo crap
i'd not believe the pitches
i won't allow me that

chorus

4. so i accept the tablet
and the pusher too
and everything i pay him
proves what he says is true

(iv)

have faith
& the evidence
is raining butterflies
a complexity
incredible
beyond the mind
creativity

have fear
& the evidence
rings inside your ingsoc
the terror
unseeable beasts
beyond your cage
incredible
welling fear intensity
the insanity
of reality deny

fear without faith
loud cowardice
that's all

those who pummel the real
disregard faith
for if they had faith
the real
would be glory

they claim their god
a trickster
a fossil planting trickster
go figure who
their fear
has them
really
unknowingly
adore

(v)

at the plastic neat
guesthouse
breakfast table

"i listened
i voted"
i said

"you listened
you voted"
she sneered

she fixtured long ago
won't hear the counterfacts
that contradict belief

(vi)

a dog
feet curled
every office man

dog foughts
bipedal refs
bitten separate

how the torch
down the stress
raise the root

howling sonata
barking majestic
whining tinnitus

up the intense
play create
up the produce

fight or bark
spoor metro
rat to crushed

the word the world [B]

(i)

greater
homeopat...
custome...
eedj...

(ii)

belief in the
—changed
snip—the did

the word was
—wasn't

language
—time—
traduction
satre limit
ours—we are

(iii)

science is
science
is
closer
science
closer is
closer
science
science to
closer to
science word
the word
unaltered
closer is
to
the unaltered
science
closer to
science closer
unaltered word
of the
science
closer
unaltered
word
of

(iv)

the best from
of language
poetry

we
be represent
of best

any word of
we
not poetry
not
the word
of we
of

(v)

the weakness
not the word
the language

the humanity
the language

the strength

(vi)

anyone
claims
knows
the word of
we

claims
ahead head
bigger
bigger than
all
all
all there is

confuse
knowledge
pride

wild justice

(i)

the wild corpse
self lost to entropy
injury killing clear
under dust

keened
that's what the watcher did
silent keening
eyes of shock

it left
returned
brought community
eyes of mourn

one prodded
a prompt
a try
for waken

keened
that's what the watchers did
silent keening
eyes of shock

and the shock blunted
mourning
slowly to be
let the living live

they flew
all of them
the living
they flew

the corpse
the wild injustice
funeral
magpie

(ii)

legs
a withered leg
legs
to move
to speed
she couldn't
a withered leg

and he
blunder and grease
this he
under the lust
of presume
bounded
and charged
and bounced
played the tank
under the lust

she fell
injured
she fell
withered leg
she fell
injured
she fell

and he
blunder and grease
this he
under the lust
of presume
bounded
and charged
and bounced
played the tank
under the lust

an old lady
the witch
the matriach
the great
an old lady
the witch
the great
the matriach

she saw
trumpeted
saw off
she saw
trumpeted
saw him off
dismissal
she saw
saw off
she saved

guarded
the young
picked up
stood
can't stand
stood unsteady
stood
must stand
unsteady
withered
can stand
must stand
stand
stood

the old lady
the witch
the matriach
the great
touched
the withered leg
protected
the withered leg
guarded
the withered leg
guarded
the young
guarded

(iii)

there
they're trapped
they'll harmed

i don't want to see the
suffering
i can't stand the sea of
suffering
i don't want to hear their
suffering

there
they're trapped
they'll hurt

that trap
i know that trap
i've seen that trap undone

there
they're trapped
they'll hurt

i don't want to see the
suffering
i can't stand the sea of
suffering
i don't want to hear their
suffering

there
they're trapped
they'll hurt

lift the metal branch
turn the metal bush
they'll walk beyond

i won't see the suffering
i won't stand the suffering
i won't hear their suffering

elephant
rescues
antelope

(iv)

if bones muscle
other mechanical
evolved

the control
the behaviour
evolved

so why not
liaison behaviour
the order of all
the morès
evolved

we together
we rose together
in animal justice

they together
they rose together
in animal justice

serotonin
morality
justice

An Apology (that makes itself necessary)

A lot of the material behind this poetry has been inspired by my reading of popular science, and popular science-fiction. I make no pretence of any effort of accuracy, nor respect to the source material, but I am going to mention some of the items so anyone who wants to explore can go google and trouser the original.

Before I go any further, I'll mention that I'm very aware that science & technology both progress, and much of what I mention in here, all those things that inspired me, may well come across as trivial and tired to future readers, presuming future readers. Well, sod you, I find your Wrapp–Flangle autocrotchet mechanical cat to be dull, too, so there. I am of my time, and this work is full of it.

Hymnen Technical Note misnames the theory that it promptly abuses, and abuses in spades, I might add. Since Hugh Everett III's *Many–Worlds Interpretation* there has been many more works in a lot of physics suggesting many different categories of parallel universe, most of which are probably real. It's far too exciting to cover here; go look up *Multiverse* in a popular online encyclopaedia. Incidentally, I suspect Hugh Everett's life story could inspire a gloriously gnarly characterisation.

I reference another category of parallel universe, *branes* from *M–Theory*. The puns are kindly provided by the scientists, and are far too good (and playgroundish) not to steal. As I write, *M–Theory* is so incomplete that it mostly consists of "This Space Is Reserved For M–Theory". Oh, go look it up; I've abused a theory again.

Underlying this poetry is a mistake I made, the same many make, of presuming that because much contemporary computer technology is split into hardware and software (and never mind field-programmable gate arrays), so it must always be so. It is, here, the same mistake as separation of mind and body, and, in the same way, the same mistake as the separation of man and machine.

I no longer agree with myself. I now understand the mind is the flesh, the way it's self-organised, and what they make. You're not your atoms, you're not the way they dance, you're what the dance produces.

I once worked with an Australian company which makes devices to be surgical implanted to restore some hearing to people with certain forms of deafness. Does substituting technology for flesh reduce those peoples' humanity? Of course not. It restores human experience, and, to those born deaf, changes it (which has caused some interesting cultural debates). Just extend that thought to thought itself. To be human is not just something more than meat space, it's beyond meat space — one day, maybe. Such explorations about what it is to be human are just one reason I consume science-fiction.

Many wonderful and clever and glorious science-fiction stories of my time contain intelligent starships which are entirely artificial beings. That's no longer my opinion. I prefer to believe they'll be people with go really faster stripes: well, and a few more things. We won't live as pets in some future culture ruled by machines we ancestored, we'll thrive in a multiverse as man-machines. The German musicians (et al) will be right, not the anglophone novelists, not this poet.

When I had youth (decades ago), I found myself researching artificial intelligence (AI). I knew the threat reputation that AIs possessed in science-fiction, the non-human super mind, and I wondered whether I might be helping bring that jelly day fear to reality (with that glorious ego of youth). So I did considered how they might actually work. My simplistic thought experiment plonked them in a place where they had to survive, where they had to do their thing, where they could not communicate effectively with their originators. They would be there by design, not by accident, not by competition. From that, I tried to work out how I might compose such minds so they could thrive.

And the outcome? Well, go read the poems: they're the only real result of my research. I wasn't the best of students, unless you're a brewery owner. I got distracted by politics, then undistracted myself when I realised I was too much of a nerd for devious pretty company.

Mind you, politics taught me that, while emotions can identify problems to address, they offer dire solutions. In a safe society like modern British society, the primary emotion is cowardice. I am British. My fears, too, were of imaginary things.

Here, poetry is brilliant. It finds those sources, and cooks them. My poetry is ash.

More than a few poems were fired up by articles on *The Simulation Argument,* put forward by the Oxford philosopher Nick Bostrom. I won't misrepresent his position here (I've already abused it enough in the poetry), beyond saying that his argument is that the maths pretty well forces us to accept we're living in a simulation: Plato's shadows for our times, perhaps. I ran with it, tripped, and fell off a cliff.

Rest In Peace, Mr. Iain Banks, I stole & perverted many ideas from you and your fellow authors. Rest In Peace, too, Herr Karlheinz Stockhausen. You kindly gave me permission to reuse the title of one of your great pieces (a postcard I subsequently lost, annoyingly), which played as I wrote the early drafts, so long ago: so many people, so much loneliness. In these poems, too, lie Dougal Dixon's beautiful *After Man.*

Tomasz Tarchała reminded me I stole the word *metaverse* from Neil Stephenson's *Snow Crash.* I read the book some time ago, but had consciously forgotten it. This might explain why I find I've extended the original meaning, twice, adding ambiguity, twice. What? You want to know what where? Hey, go read the poetry!

A more recent misinterpretation of mine concerns *The Holographic Principle,* which, at the time of writing, is a useful mathematical trick to make some dastardly theoretical physics calculations somewhat easier, but which fires up the popular press to produce some delicious nonsense. The trick pretends that, although we might think we're living in a 3D universe, we're really merely a mess of interference patterns on the 2D interior surface of the skin of a black hole. It might even be more than an algebraic trick. Go look it up, I've made enough mess of the explanation already.

my father was a ufo

my father was a ufo
eating passengers for tea
afore he went to bed
he ran the tale of me

my father was an aircraft ship
his arm around the sea
afore he went to bed
he ran the tale of me

my father was a hobbit dwarf
making myth for thee
afore he went to bed
he ran the tale of me

my father was the emperor
of factory 63
afore he went to bed
he ran the tale of me

my father was the counter–ghost
he warmed the winds of plea
afore he went to bed
he ran the tale of me

my father's post computer
from the singularity
before he builds his birthing bed
he'll run the tale of me

It isn't just incredible ideas from physics that have led me on. I encountered a book on animal social behaviour, *Wild Justice,* that got me going so much I stole the title and the content for some poems. I was shocked to discover some animals have morals, yet Marc Bekoff and Jessica Pierce made such a good case that I have became convinced. As I write, this is not a matter of consensus amongst biologists, but, heck, this book is poetry, not a paper. Well, it is paper. Er, on paper. Might be. You know what I mean. Bah! :-)

The poem, *my father was a ufo* travels in the same place as the motivation for the poetry here, but doesn't belong among them. It travels in the same space as the characters here, but they don't know it. The poem is not in the book. It is the sole of the book. It is the motto of The Church of All Our Soles. It is a recursive lie. It is the truth. The best lie is the truth.

I should acknowledge certain poetic influences. The dominant has to be Cambridge, both town and gown. I was never gown (I'm a Thames Polytechnic survivor), but the coattails are delicious. The *Cambridge Conference of Contemporary Poetry* opened my poetry world. I thank its organisers, and the organisers of similar conferences, heartily. The works of *Drew Milne* and others made me confident being seen to mix science into poetry, even though I'd been doing it since *Broadside* in Birmingham, where *Hymnen* was first written. This work could not exist without them, nor many others.

I hope it's clear by now that I find both science and technology fun. I've tried to show this. They're both transient, even for the great ideas. I've tried to express that, too, and more, in this essay's writing style.

Most of all, though, both technology and science are sodding difficult. It's so easy to travel the simple road, the freeway to Get It Completely Wrong. That, most of all, has to be addressed, has to be admitted. This poetry hares down Easy Street. That's why this apology is necessary, is here, is what it is, reflecting what I read into the subject, reflecting what I feel about it, confessing my myriad failures. Indeed, the only people who don't admit failures in their understanding of science and technology are those who don't.

The first step to understanding is acceptance that you don't, and doing something about it. So is the next step. So are them all.

The errors in my understanding of the science and technology are nothing to do with the original material. They're mine, all mine! It really doesn't help that I love the way imperfections corrupt their subject. Anyway, if anything is actually right, it only shows that even a staggering idiot can sometimes fail to fall over.

Seriously, I hope you've enjoyed what's here. What?! Bah! :-)

– Dylan Harris Luxembourg Christmas 2013

Also by Dylan Harris

Poetry:

antwerp, (wurm press)

europe, (wurm press)

Poetry & photography:

the liberation of [placeholder], (The Knives, Forks and Spoons Press)

the smoke, (The Knives, Forks and Spoons Press)

Photography:

plein, (corrupt press)

la défense, (corrupt press)

Recording:

the DVD chapbook (privately distributed).

Music:

flock state (Tunecore, as devon garde)

Web:

dylanharris.org.